Knight

Contents	Page
Castles	2-3
Parts of the castle	4-5
Workers in the castle	6-7
The great hall	8-9
An attack	10-11
Training to be a knight	12-13
Armor	14-15
Tournaments and jousting	16-17
Hawking and the coat of arms	18-19
Gunpowder and castles today	20-21
King Arthur and knights of the round table	22-23
Index	24

written by John Lockyer

About a thousand ago, towering castles were built all across Europe. Most of them were fortified with huge inner and outer walls made from thick stone. Some of them were surrounded by a moat – a deep, steep-sided ditch full of water. The only way to get into these castles was by crossing a drawbridge, which was raised during an attack. High turrets were watch towers to guard against invaders.

In those days, the castle was the home of a lord. It was also the home of knights, soldiers, crafts-people and many servants. The lord and his family lived in the Great Tower. The castle was a busy place. Everything needed for daily life was made or found in the castle, or on the land around it.

The bailey (or courtyard) was an open space in the middle of the castle. Markets were held there. Merchants and farmers living nearby came to sell or trade animals, crops and goods. Markets were also a time for people to share news and have fun.

In and around the castle, workers grew crops and looked after sheep and cattle. Spinners and weavers made clothes. Woodworkers built furniture and blacksmiths crafted tools, weapons and armor. At the same time, servants gardened, washed clothes, chopped firewood, fetched water from the well, swept and cleaned floors and prepared food. Feeding everyone in a castle was a huge job. Cooking was done in large kitchens over open fires. Most of the food was boiled or roasted on a spit. When the food was ready it was carried into the Great Hall.

A blacksmith at work

The Great Hall was the main room in the castle. Tapestries hung on the walls and sweet-smelling reeds covered the floor. At meal times, the lord and his guests sat near a blazing fire. The less important people sat at the other end of the room. Everyone ate with their fingers.

After the meal, there was entertainment. Minstrels sang, jesters made jokes, storytellers told tales and actors presented plays. Later, the lord left the Great Hall to sleep in the tower. Everyone else wrapped themselves in blankets and slept on the floor.

A feast for a lord

The castle was protected during the day and at night by soldiers. They guarded prisoners in the dungeons. They checked everyone who came into the castle and they patrolled the parapet. The high turrets gave them a good view of any attackers.

During a raid, enemies used battering rams, catapults and wooden towers to storm the castle. The lord and his soldiers fought back with bows and arrows, firing through narrow slits in the walls. They lowered the portcullis (a strong spiked gate) to block the entrance, and dropped boiling liquids and huge rocks onto anyone trying to get over the walls.

Knights also defended the castle. They rode into battle on huge warhorses. They used lances, swords and maces to attack their enemies. They were expert fighting men who started their training when they were only seven years old.

A boy who was chosen to become a knight was called a page. When he turned fourteen, he became a squire and went to live with a real knight to learn to fight with his hands and hunt with a bow. He also had practice with different weapons and looked after his knight's horses. A squire even went into battle with his knight.

A squire became a knight when he was about twenty-one. Kneeling before his lord, family and friends, he made the knight's promise:
- to keep his word,
- to look after the weak
- to serve his lord.

Many lords rewarded their knights' bravery and loyalty with land and treasure.

To protect themselves in battle, knights wore steel armor. Armor covered the head, chest, back, legs and feet. Chain mail was worn under the armor to give the knight even more protection. Some knights' armor was so heavy that they had to be lifted onto their horses.

Jousting

During peace time, knights still needed practice of their fighting skills. Sometimes a lord invited knights from other castles to a grand tournament. At the tournament, the knights split into two teams and fought each other in a mock battle. The defeated knights had to give their horses and armor to the winners. Jousting was also popular at tournaments. Large crowds gathered in a field to watch the knights, carrying lances, charging toward each other at top speed. The knight who knocked his opponent off his horse with one blow was the winner of a joust.

Most knights also had a hawk or falcon for the hawking contest. These fierce birds of prey were trained to catch small animals such as ducks, rabbits and pheasants.

At tournaments and in battle, the knights were almost completely covered in armor. So that everyone knew who was who, each knight had a different coat of arms. The knight chose his own colours, patterns and symbols for his coat of arms. Eagles, dragons, lions and unicorns were popular symbols. The coat of arms was displayed on the knight's costume, shield, flag and on his horse's robe.

During the 1500s, castles became dangerous places to defend. Gunpowder changed the way battles were fought. Huge cannonballs destroyed the castles' walls. Bows and arrows were no match for muskets or pistols. Many lords left their castles and built smaller manor houses. With no lord, soldiers or knights to protect them, the people left too.

Although most castles became ruins, some castles are still lived in today. Many of them are open to the public. Visitors can discover what life was like six hundred years ago for a lord, his knights and his people.

There are many legends about castles, kings, lords and knights. The story of King Arthur is one of the greatest. With Merlin the Magician as his protector, and Excalibur, his magical sword, Arthur became a brave, wise and powerful king.
Arthur lived at the castle of Camelot with Queen Guinevere and his Knights of the Round Table. Sir Lancelot, Sir Galahad, Sir Gawain and King Arthur's other knights fought dragons, rescued princesses, protected the weak and searched for lost treasures.

Index	Page
armor	14
coat of arms	18
drawbridge	2
dungeon	10
Excalibur	22
Great Tower	4
Great Hall	6,8
joust	17
King Arthur	22
knights	4, 12, 14-22
lord	4, 8, 10, 20, 22
Merlin the Magician	22
page	12
soldiers	10
squire	12,14
turret	2
weapons	10, 12, 20